Protecting America

U.S. Customs and Border Protection

2005–2010 Strategic Plan

U.S. Customs and
Border Protection

The terrorist attacks of 9/11 challenged us in ways we had never before experienced. The agency's mission and its future were dramatically altered that day. Our priority mission changed to a national security mission: preventing terrorists and terrorist weapons from entering the United States. Also understood was the significance of securing our borders without choking the flow of legitimate trade and travel – all while continuing to carry out the traditional missions of the predecessor agencies that make up U.S. Customs and Border Protection.

- Commissioner Robert C. Bonner

Testimony before the National Commission on Terrorist Attacks Upon the United States

Message from the Commissioner

One of the most important concepts of the Homeland Security reorganization was the creation of one border agency for the United States; one agency to manage, control and secure our nation's borders. Concurrent with the creation of the Department of Homeland Security (DHS), U.S. Customs and Border Protection (CBP) was established and placed under the Department's Border and Transportation Security Directorate (BTS). By combining the immigration, customs and agricultural border inspection functions together, with the Border Patrol and its functions between the ports of entry, CBP became the single federal agency principally responsible for managing and securing our nation's borders both at and between the ports of entry. For the first time, one United States border agency is in a position to develop and implement a comprehensive strategy for border security and enforcement of all laws at our borders.

After 9/11, CBP understood that we must increase the security of our borders, but we needed to do this without unduly stifling the flow of legitimate trade and travel into our country. Indeed, through innovative programs we have demonstrated that it is possible to facilitate the movement of goods and people while also increasing security of our borders, so undeniably necessary in the post 9/11 era of global terrorism. We have protected our nation with our pioneering "Smart Borders" and extended border strategies, and we have protected our economy as well. We have done this - and will continue to do this - by moving forward on the initiatives set in motion after 9/11.

This FY 2005–2010 Strategic Plan sets out a vision for CBP. It delineates the strategic goals and objectives that CBP must achieve to be successful at carrying out its extraordinarily important mission while facilitating the flow of legitimate trade and travel through our ports of entry.

Commissioner Robert C. Bonner

Protecting America

U.S. Customs and Border Protection

2005–2010 Strategic Plan

Contents

Executive Summary

The priority mission of the U.S. Customs and Border Protection (CBP) is homeland security. For the border agency charged with managing, securing and controlling the nation's border, that means the CBP priority mission is to prevent terrorists and terrorist weapons from entering the United States. The strategic intent of the FY 2005–2010 Strategic Plan reflects this priority mission.

An important aspect of this mission involves improving security both at and between United States ports of entry, but it also means extending the zone of security beyond the physical borders. This extended border strategy is essential to creating smart borders and a layered defense-in-depth strategy.

To become more effective and efficient in accomplishing its mission, CBP is unifying as one border agency. By integrating all of the federal inspection elements at the ports of entry with the Border Patrol, CBP will form a unified border agency within DHS. CBP will create an agency-wide law enforcement and national security culture, establish unified primary inspection at all United States ports of entry and conduct specialized secondary inspections focused on combating terrorism.

While carrying out its priority mission, CBP must also work to facilitate the movement of legitimate trade and people. The agency will accomplish its facilitation goals by gathering advance data regarding incoming and outgoing people, conveyances and goods; improving targeting; and using technology to leverage its resources. CBP will also promote government and private sector partnerships that permit screening of cargo and people beyond United States borders.

In addition to its priority mission, CBP will work to protect America and its citizens by carrying out

its traditional missions more effectively using innovative approaches. These traditional missions include enforcing United States trade, immigration and other laws at the borders. Trade-related mission activities include protecting American businesses from theft of their intellectual property and unfair trade practices; regulating and facilitating international trade; collecting import duties; enforcing trade laws related to admissibility; regulating trade practices to collect the appropriate revenue; and maintaining export controls. Other traditional missions include controlling the borders by apprehending individuals attempting to enter the United States illegally; stemming the flow of illegal drugs and other contraband; protecting agriculture and economic interests from harmful pests and diseases; processing all people, vehicles and cargo entering the United States; and coordinating with the Department of Defense and others to protect the National Capital Region.

None of these priorities can be accomplished without a strong and effective management support structure that assures the achievement of "business" results. This infrastructure includes effective financial systems, quality recruitment, a skilled and diverse workforce, enhanced information flow, continued roll out of the Automated Commercial Environment (ACE) and the use of integrated, cutting-edge technologies.

CBP accepts and embraces its responsibilities to protect America, its citizens, and the economy. The FY 2005–2010 Strategic Plan provides the direction and framework to carry out this critical role.

Photo: CBP Honor Guard preparing to fold the Flag 3

CBP Mission Statement

We are the guardians of our nation's borders.

We are America's frontline.

We safeguard the American homeland at and beyond our borders.

We protect the American public against terrorists and the instruments of terror.

We steadfastly enforce the laws of the United States while fostering our nation's economic security through lawful international trade and travel.

We serve the American public with vigilance, integrity and professionalism.

CBP core values reflect the dedication and professionalism of its workforce.

Vigilance

Vigilance is how we ensure the safety of all Americans. We are continuously watchful and alert to deter, detect and prevent threats to our nation. We demonstrate courage and valor in the protection of our nation.

Service to Country

Service to Country is embodied in the work we do. We are dedicated to defending and upholding the Constitution of the United States. The American people have entrusted us to protect the homeland and defend liberty.

Integrity

Integrity is our cornerstone. We are guided by the highest ethical and moral principles. Our actions bring honor to ourselves and our agency.

Background/Legislative History

To help the nation meet the threat of international terrorism, President George W. Bush signed the Homeland Security Act of 2002, thus beginning the most extensive reorganization of the federal government since the 1940s. It also provided for a change that has been advocated by every study of border agencies conducted over the past 30 years. For the first time in this country's history, all agencies with significant border responsibilities have been integrated and unified into a single organization responsible for managing, controlling and securing the nation's borders. This landmark legislation consolidated functions from 22 federal agencies.

CBP was established as one of three operational agencies within the Border and Transportation Security Directorate. CBP consists of the inspection and frontline border enforcement functions of the U.S. Customs Service, the Immigration and Naturalization Service (INS), including the Border Patrol, and the Animal and Plant Health Inspection Service (APHIS). It also includes all of the trade and revenue collection functions of the U.S. Customs Service. The predecessor agencies each have rich histories and missions that they bring to CBP. But today, as part of the historic creation of a unified agency, the priority mission of all CBP personnel is to detect and prevent terrorists and terrorist weapons from entering the United States.

Through CBP, the nation will realize the benefits of integrated inspection and border resources. These benefits include more effective security and the facilitation of legitimate people and goods across the border to promote economic security by establishing a unified border agency. And, while CBP continues to carry out the traditional roles of its predecessor agencies, and build on their rich traditions and histories, CBP is forging a new agency within the Department of Home-

Photo: President Bush applauds Secretary Michael Chertoff after he was sworn in as the 2nd Secretary of DHS

land Security. It is the dawn of a new era – where, as one border agency, CBP can, and will, more effectively and efficiently strengthen commerce while strengthening America's borders.

Photo: Secretary Chertoff and Commissioner Bonner at Dulles Airport

Threat and Vulnerability

U.S. Customs and Border Protection (CBP), in its capacity as the frontline border security agency, faces a significant terrorist threat at air, land and sea ports of entry, as well as between the ports of entry. The vast length of United States borders provides opportunities for drug trafficking, alien smuggling and other criminal activities, including terrorist networks. The threat to the national security of the United States and CBP manifests itself primarily in the potential for regular and repeated encounters with foreign terrorists and their conveyances as they enter the United States, both at and between the ports of entry. Those encounters are the result of terrorists' travel and shipments of material to support their organization in the United States and abroad.

According to testimony by Intelligence Community officials to the Senate, al Qaeda and affiliated Sunni extremists continue to pose a strategic threat to the homeland and remain intent on carrying out another attack in the United States. The consensus among the Intelligence Community agencies is that another terrorist attack is "inevitable." International counterterrorism successes have made it more difficult for al Qaeda to operate, but they remain resolute in their objectives. There have been multiple efforts to target the homeland since 9/11, including Richard Reid's attempted shoe bomb attack against a commercial airliner and Jose Padilla's dirty bomb plot.

The intention of al Qaeda is to achieve maximum casualties in a spectacular manner, and they want the next attack on United States soil to surpass that of 9/11. Conventional explosives and improvised explosive devices (IEDs) continue to be the mainstay of al Qaeda tactics. However, al Qaeda has increased its efforts to study, experiment with and seek chemical, biological and radiological agents. Additionally, the al Qaeda network continues to be interested in attacks involving

Photo: President Bush praises CBP employees and discusses Homeland Security in Washington, DC

commercial aviation. Targets may include financial districts, hotels, tourist sites, apartment buildings, subways and symbols of the United States government such as the White House and the Pentagon.

Al Qaeda continues to look for ways to circumvent U.S. security enhancements to strike Americans and the homeland, as evidenced by the plan to exploit the now defunct Transit Without Visa (TWOV) Program in 2003. As part of this strategy, al Qaeda has also been recruiting "non-traditional" operatives that would draw less suspicion from United States border authorities. Al Qaeda will continue to look for opportunities to exploit legitimate immigration and visa policies, as well as security measures against the detection of fraudulent travel documents.

The al Qaeda network may also be seeking to exploit the capabilities of established alien and/or smuggling networks, particularly on the Southwest Border. The recent testimony to the Senate also included statements that several al Qaeda leaders believe that terrorist operatives can pay their way into the United States from Mexico. Additionally, some may prefer to make illegal entry as many known al Qaeda operatives have been placed on government watch lists.

Although al Qaeda and affiliated Sunni extremist groups pose the greatest threat to the United States, other terrorist groups also pose persistent and serious threats to United States interests. Of these other groups, Hizballah poses the biggest potential threat, as it could conduct lethal attacks against United States interests quickly should they decide to do so.

The global threat posed by terrorism, at home and abroad, continues to impact nearly all aspects of international security, trade and commerce. The commercial maritime domain may be most at risk from exploitation by terrorists, potentially resulting in massive disruptions to global economies. Increased terrorist calls for attacks specifically against Western economic targets, as well as growing indications of terrorist intentions to use weapons of mass destruction, highlight the assessed likelihood that maritime trade will remain a tool of choice to support or carry out such attacks. Current intelligence indicates that, of the various potential terrorist choices for weapons of mass destruction, a radiological dispersal device ("dirty bomb") or chemical weapons agent may be the most likely and both are well-suited to smuggling via sea container. An al Qaeda plot to smuggle explosives in containers to the United States was revealed in 2003 with the detainment of Saifullah Paracha, a Pakistani businessman who ran an import/export business in New York.

Terrorist organizations continue to target our socio-economic infrastructure and pursue weapons and components. Given the enormity of the consequences posed, a comprehensive strategy for protecting America is imperative. The multi-layered approach described in this Strategic Plan sets out the CBP strategy to address the global terrorist threat.

External Factors

Moving forward into the 21st Century, CBP will be dramatically influenced by a number of external global factors. To anticipate these will present formidable challenges and opportunities for CBP. The following are a few scenarios, identified through environmental scanning and futures research, that will have an impact on the agency and its ability to prepare for the future.

Combating Terrorism and Crime

Criminals hold distinct advantages over the law enforcement community by using sophisticated international criminal cooperation and the use of legitimate businesses as cover. Alliances have been developed between domestic and international terrorist organizations. Terrorists use established smuggling and illegal immigration routes, and direct links have been established between terrorism, drug and arms trafficking, money laundering and counterfeiting. The capability of criminals to leverage technology to conduct and hide crimes, and to leverage social concerns for privacy and justice, brings frustration and challenges for the law enforcement community. With more intensive antiterrorism inspections at ports of entry, there will likely be an increase in interdicting narcotics, illegal aliens and foreigners with criminal backgrounds. Increased enforcement efforts at the ports of entry may also be expected to cause terrorists to shift the focus of their efforts toward identified or perceived vulnerabilities between the ports. It is also clear that because of the globalization of terrorism and crime, the government will need to collaborate with foreign partners to share information, technology and techniques to combat this threat to national and international security. Pressure will increase on the government to address this level of criminal activity including a need to monitor and control the potential intentional disruption of natural resources such as domestically grown agricultural products and water supplies, as well as imported food.

Impact of Globalization

The safety of global trade is both an economic issue and a security concern. A weapon of mass destruction or weapon of mass effect, detonated at a United States port of entry, could cause a $1 trillion disruption to the economy. With the continued expansion of globalization, trade will increase and bring more diverse product design and production methods, more stakeholders and modes of transportation, and with all of this, criminals and terrorists. CBP, as well as other government agencies, will have difficulty creating equitable, effective trade rules because of a growing world population and the corresponding purchasing power associated with growth, trade liberalization and uncertain product valuation due to cross-border production and intellectual capital. More duty-free goods will reduce tariffs and revenue collection but will require increased oversight to ensure eligibility for decreased duty rates. The future also means more trade agreements, and CBP will use state-of-the-art technologies to help better target for high risks, employing other means for enforcement that reach beyond stopping cargo at time of entry. The agency is committed to swift and strong enforcement actions to deter repeat violations. To fight illegal trade practices, the government must continue inspecting for illegal imports and enforcing trade laws. Foreign governments, shippers, vendors and the trade community will be relied upon for collecting and sharing information and will also need to assure that processes are secure.

Facilitating Trade and Travel While Ensuring Security and Safety

CBP will continue to face the challenge of enhancing a system to keep terrorists and their weapons out of the United States while facilitating trade. CBP will need more efficient ways to move freight securely. Working with Canada and Mexico, CBP will pursue tightening border security while trying to reduce delays and improve relations. While continued global migration means more diverse international passenger travel, the public will expect speedy, consistent processing and demand safety and security. Global trade needs for tailored, speedy delivery will require more deep-water ports, more virtual ports with online processing and an increase in all types of freight, larger trucks and bigger container ships. Passenger and shipper needs for quick and efficient movement of goods will generate more processing at non-border locations and create more entry points inland using an automated infrastructure and intelligent highway systems with imbedded sensors to allow automatic vehicle traffic.

Technology and Inventions

Linking disparate databases, communication systems and other technologies of the 22 agencies and partners that make up DHS will be a continuous, evolutionary process for the foreseeable future. Innovative technology solutions for monitoring, inspection, information sharing and enforcement will grow, but will also bring implementation and standardization challenges. A new electronic system for tracking cargo coming into ports will save both shippers and the United States government money, but will require investments by the trade community. Technologies and processes will offer opportunities to deter misdeeds, facilitate enforcement and better value goods. Advanced technology and a distributed, open, wireless and mobile environment will be available to CBP, but technological advances and new products will also challenge the workforce requiring different skill sets.

The Millennium Workforce

Challenges facing agencies transitioning to, and integrating into, DHS include building and adopting the new culture, setting priorities and training employees. A unified border agency means that the core occupations will change, requiring the development of new occupations and combining and integrating the efforts of the CBP frontline workforce while ensuring adequate staffing and training. In addition, the more general challenges of the 21st Century involve growing workforce complexity, diversity, mobility, continual training, instant electronic connectivity and independence. Trends and priorities impacting federal managers include retirements, downsizing, information technology advances, contracting reforms and aging staffs. CBP will need more innovative recruiting, retention and reinvigoration/training programs, along with refined knowledge management processes and advanced law enforcement technologies. Federal managers will continue to face pressures to view the public as customers, to measure program performance and results and to justify new projects and investments with business cases. To ensure the government can prevent and respond to threats of domestic security, federal managers must be able to maintain and upgrade the critical infrastructures needed to accomplish the CBP mission and strategic goals.

Meeting the Challenge

CBP is steeped in tradition and committed to serving the public. In anticipation of the challenges and opportunities the future will bring, this Strategic Plan serves as the framework to assure that the agency is prepared to protect the nation and the economy.

Strategic Planning Process

The CBP comprehensive strategic planning process is driven by the need to address the global challenges to a secure homeland and economy. The CBP FY 2005–2010 Strategic Plan is based on the priorities that were established and articulated by the Secretary, Homeland Security; the Under Secretary, Border and Transportation Security; and the Commissioner of Customs and Border Protection. The Strategic Plan is prepared with input from senior managers to reflect these priorities and ties directly to the budgets prepared by CBP. The development process has considered the DHS Strategic Plan, the National Strategy for Homeland Security, the National Money Laundering Strategy, the National Drug Control Strategy, Presidential Directives on National Security and Executive Orders. In addition, the President's Management Agenda (PMA), budget justification materials, internal strategic planning initiatives and the DHS Future Year Homeland Security Program (FYHSP), used for formulating, analyzing and reporting the DHS planning and budgeting process, were considered. Finally, evaluations conducted through the Government Accountability Office (GAO), the Office of the Inspector General (OIG) and the Performance Assessment Rating Tool (PART) processes have also been assessed.

The CBP strategic planning framework is organized as follows:

- **Strategic goal:**
  A high level statement of what needs to be achieved;

Photo: Numerous agencies both within and outside DHS collaborate to secure the borders

- ***Objectives:***
  Specific statements of what is to be accomplished within the goal;

- ***Strategies:***
  Specific actions that are to be taken to reach an objective; and

- ***Performance measures:***
  What will be accomplished by carrying out the strategies.

Each strategic goal is presented using the CBP strategic planning framework, and each strategic goal was determined based on future assumptions, previous accomplishments and the need to integrate diverse CBP responsibilities effectively. The goals are further linked to specific objectives and strategies, as well as performance measures that are used to measure progress toward achieving the goals. This strategic planning process has resulted in the formulation of six strategic goals and associated objectives and strategies. These goals are described below.

1. Preventing Terrorism At Ports of Entry:

Prevent terrorists and terrorist weapons, including weapons of mass destruction and weapons of mass effect, from entering the United States at the ports of entry.

2. Preventing Terrorism Between Ports of Entry:

Strengthen control of the borders between the ports of entry to prevent the illegal entry of terrorists, terrorist weapons, contraband and illegal aliens into the United States.

3. Unifying As One Border Agency:

Increase the security of the homeland by completing the merger and unification of all United States border agencies.

4. Facilitating Legitimate Trade and Travel:

Facilitate the more efficient movement of legitimate cargo and people.

5. Protecting America and Its Citizens:

Contribute to a safer America by prohibiting the introduction of illicit contraband, such as illegal drugs, counterfeit goods and other harmful materials and organisms, into the United States.

6. Modernizing and Managing:

Continue to build a strong, modern infrastructure that assures the achievement of business results.

By achieving these goals through partnerships with government agencies, the private sector and foreign governments, CBP will advance DHS goals and its mission to protect the United States against attacks and threats to the homeland. In addition, these goals form a cornerstone of the DHS FYHSP system and link directly to DHS goals as shown in the following chart.

CBP/DHS Strategic Goals Crosswalk

CBP Strategic Goals	Objectives	DHS Strategic Goals			
		Prevention — Detect, deter and mitigate threats to the homeland.			**Service** — Serve the public by facilitating lawful travel, trade and immigration.
		2.1: Secure the borders against terrorists, means of terrorism, illegal drugs and violations of trade and immigration laws.	2.3: Provide end users with technology and capabilities to detect/prevent terrorism and other illegal activities.	3.1: Protect the Public from acts of terrorism and other illegal activities.	6.4: Facilitate the legitimate movement of cargo and people.
1 Preventing Terrorism At Ports of Entry: Prevent terrorists and terrorist weapons, including weapons of mass destruction and weapons of mass effect, from entering the United States.	1.1: Improve the collection, use, analysis and dissemination of intelligence to target, identify and prevent potential terrorists and terrorist weapons from entering the United States.	✖	✖		
	1.2: Improve identification and targeting of potential terrorists and terrorist weapons, through risk management and automated advanced and enhanced information.	✖	✖		
	1.3: Strengthen the CBP defense-in-depth approach through the use of state-of-the-art detection and sensor technology, resources and training.	✖	✖		
	1.4: Push the nation's zone of security beyond physical U.S. borders through partnerships and extended border initiatives to deter and combat the threat of terrorism.	✖	✖		
2 Preventing Terrorism Between Ports of Entry: Strengthen the control of the borders between the ports of entry to prevent the illegal entry of terrorists, terrorist weapons, contraband, and illegal aliens into the United States.	2.1: Enhance the intelligence program, and improve intelligence-driven operations.	✖	✖		
	2.2: Maximize border security, along the northern, southern and coastal borders, through an appropriate balance of personnel, equipment, technology, communications capabilities and tactical infrastructure.	✖	✖		
	2.3: Expand specialized teams and rapid-response capabilities to enhance control of the borders, with expansion to problematic areas as identified through continuing threat assessments.	✖			
	2.4: Develop a more flexible, well-trained, nationally directed program and address central infrastructure, facility and technology needs.	✖			

CBP/DHS Strategic Goals Crosswalk			DHS Strategic Goals			
			Prevention Detect, deter and mitigate threats to the homeland.			**Service** Serve the public by facilitating lawful travel, trade and immigration.
CBP Strategic Goals		Objectives	2.1: Secure the borders against terrorists, means of terrorism, illegal drugs and violations of trade and immigration laws.	2.3: Provide end users with technology and capabilities to detect/prevent terrorism and other illegal activities.	3.1: Protect the Public from acts of terrorism and other illegal activities.	6.4: Facilitate the legitimate movement of cargo and people.
3	*Unifying as One Border Agency:*					
	Increase the security of the homeland by completing the merger and unification of all United States border agencies.	3.1: Create a shared law enforcement culture throughout the agency to secure the homeland.	✖			
		3.2: Develop and implement policy, management, operations, infrastructure and training initiatives to integrate frontline border enforcement personnel.	✖			✖
		3.3: Establish a unified primary inspection process for passenger processing at all ports of entry into the United States and fully integrate analysis and targeting units.	✖	✖		✖
		3.4: Leverage the expertise, capabilities and legal authorities of CBP officers to establish antiterrorism secondary inspections.	✖	✖		
		3.5: Realign the Air and Marine Operations (AMO) to improve the overall operational effectiveness and efficiencies of CBP air and marine assets.	✖	✖	✖	
4	*Facilitating Legitimate Trade and Travel:*					
	Facilitate the more efficient movement of legitimate cargo and people.	4.1: Modernize automated import, export and passenger processing systems to improve risk assessment and enforcement decision-making.	✖	✖		✖
		4.2: Utilize state-of-the-art technologies and processes to leverage resources and to conduct examinations of all potential high-risk cargo, conveyances and passengers.	✖	✖		✖
		4.3: Promote industry and foreign government partnership programs.	✖			✖
		4.4: Enforce all U.S. trade, immigration, drug, consumer protection, intellectual property and agricultural laws and regulations at the borders.				
		4.5: Facilitate international trade and travel.	✖			✖
		4.6: Ensure revenue protection.	✖			

CBP/DHS Strategic Goals Crosswalk

		DHS Strategic Goals			
		Prevention Detect, deter and mitigate threats to the homeland.			**Service** Serve the public by facilitating lawful travel, trade and immigration.
CBP Strategic Goals	**Objectives**	2.1: Secure the borders against terrorists, means of terrorism, illegal drugs and violations of trade and immigration laws.	2.3: Provide end users with technology and capabilities to detect/prevent terrorism and other illegal activities.	3.1: Protect the Public from acts of terrorism and other illegal activities.	6.4: Facilitate the legitimate movement of cargo and people.
5 *Protecting America and Its Citizens:* Contribute to a safer America by prohibiting the introduction of illicit contraband, such as illegal drugs, counterfeit goods and other harmful materials and organisms, into the United States.	5.1: Capitalize on the use of information and intelligence to identify and target the CBP enforcement response to drug trafficking, illegal immigration and other illegal activities.	✖	✖		
	5.2: Deploy automation, systems, tools and other technologies that can be used to pre-screen and identify smugglers and smuggled merchandise to increase interdiction and apprehension effectiveness.	✖	✖		
	5.3: Cooperate with other agencies, foreign governments and industry partners to administer and enforce the laws of the United States.	✖			
	5.4: Reduce the importation of all prohibited or illegal drugs and other materials that are harmful to the public or may damage the American economy.	✖			
	5.5: Provide support to protect events and key assets of national interest, and mitigate the risks of terrorism and other threats to critical Government operations.	✖	✖	✖	
6 *Modernizing and Managing:* Build a strong, modern management infrastructure that assures the achievement of business results.	**Financial, Acquisition and Asset Management**				
	6.1: Improve budgeting and financial processes, policies and systems, ensuring accurate, reliable allocation of, and accounting for, expenditure of funds, collection of revenues and maintenance of reliable, timely and accurate financial data for decision-making and reporting.	✖			
	6.2: Improve asset acquisition and management methods and procedures, ensuring the effective procurement of supplies, services and equipment in alignment with the CBP mission, goals and priorities. Implement systems and processes to efficiently construct, maintain, distribute and dispose of assets needed to carry out the CBP operational missions.	✖			

CBP/DHS Strategic Goals Crosswalk

CBP Strategic Goals	Objectives	DHS Strategic Goals			
		Prevention — Detect, deter and mitigate threats to the homeland.			**Service** — Serve the public by facilitating lawful travel, trade and immigration.
		2.1: Secure the borders against terrorists, means of terrorism, illegal drugs and violations of trade and immigration laws.	2.3: Provide end users with technology and capabilities to detect/prevent terrorism and other illegal activities.	3.1: Protect the Public from acts of terrorism and other illegal activities.	6.4: Facilitate the legitimate movement of cargo and people.
6 Modernizing and Managing: Build a strong, modern management infrastructure that assures the achievement of business results.	**Information, Science and Technology**				
	6.3: Develop and deploy innovative and secure systems and advanced technologies including ACE, APIS, US VISIT, ATS, radiation portal monitors, NII systems and America's Shield Initiative to improve targeting and screening of goods, people and conveyances entering the United States.	✖			
	6.4: Maintain a reliable, stable and secure IT infrastructure and an array of technical support services including laboratory and scientific services, tactical radio communication, field equipment maintenance/support and 24/7 customer assistance.	✖			
	Human Capital				
	6.5: Align human resources systems with the mission to ensure that recruitment, compensation, performance management, succession management and leadership of employees support professional, timely and effective service delivery to carry out the CBP mission.	✖			
	6.6: Promote continued compliance with the nation's civil rights laws and federal regulations.	✖			
	Training and Development				
	6.7: Develop and implement training initiatives that support the agency mission and priority goals, objectives and strategies in the CBP Strategic Plan.	✖			
	Management Effectiveness				
	6.8: Conduct ongoing assessments of CBP operations to assure effective and efficient utilization of resources.	✖			

Preventing Terrorism At Ports of Entry

Strategic Goal Number 1

Prevent terrorists and terrorist weapons, including weapons of mass destruction and weapons of mass effect, from entering the United States at the ports of entry.

To achieve this strategic goal, CBP will implement the Strategic Plans for Preventing Terrorists from Entering the United States and for Preventing Terrorist Weapons from Entering the United States. Through improved targeting and intelligence, CBP will target and interdict terrorists and their weapons at the ports of entry. Through various programs, CBP screens and examines passengers, cargo and conveyances posing a potential high risk for terrorism prior to departing foreign ports for the United States. To protect legitimate travel, trade and the economy, CBP will extend its zone of security beyond the physical borders, by stationing its offices in foreign countries, and by partnering with international entities and the trade community.

Objective 1.1

Improve the collection, use, analysis and dissemination of intelligence to target, identify and prevent potential terrorists and terrorist weapons from entering the United States.

To achieve timely interdiction and enforcement actions, CBP will expand intelligence collection and dissemination, enhance information sharing capabilities and increase the rapid exchange of intelligence and information that assists frontline officers in identifying potential threats. CBP will generate tactical and proactive intelligence products and disseminate reports to the field, DHS and other federal agencies. To assist in identifying passengers, cargo or conveyances that may pose a potential threat, CBP will forward intelligence to its operational components and identify trends and patterns on a local, regional and national level. Maximizing the

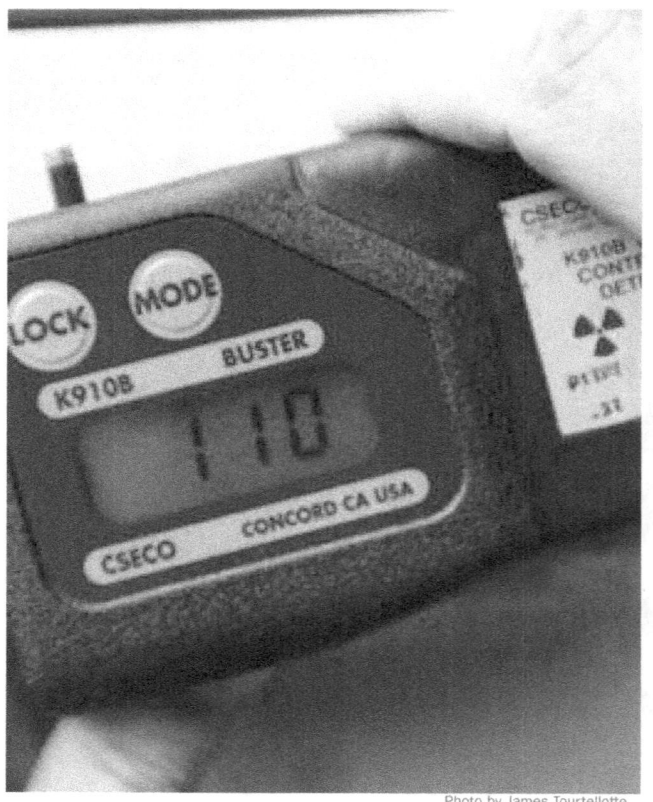

Buster measures anomalies in the density of objects

rapid exchange of terrorism-related intelligence, CBP intends to coordinate its intelligence requirements with DHS and aggressively engage intelligence community agencies, law enforcement and
military agencies, as well as foreign counterparts, including placing intelligence analysts in essential areas. CBP will also coordinate with the FBI's Joint Terrorism Task Forces (JTTFs). To provide
guidance on conducting specific operations in the field, CBP will form Intelligence Driven Special
Operations and support the Container Security Initiative (CSI) assessment teams with intelligence updates. CBP will continue a partnership with the U.S. Department of Agriculture (USDA) to
develop and use analysis and targeting to secure agricultural and economic interests from harmful
organisms and disease.

Objective 1.2

*Improve the identification and targeting of potential terrorists and terrorist weapons,
through risk management and automated advance and enhanced information.*

To improve targeting of cargo and passengers that pose a potential risk for terrorism, CBP will
continue to use advance passenger and cargo information, as well as commercial and law enforcement databases, to pre-screen, target and identify potential terrorists and terrorist shipments and
any related activity. To improve targeting and analysis, CBP will integrate existing databases and
enhance its rules-based targeting system. Through the International Trade Data System (ITDS),
CBP will provide an integrated, government-wide system to track all commerce crossing U.S. borders and to collect, use and disseminate the data required by the various trade-related federal
agencies. The CBP National Targeting Center (NTC) will provide tactical targeting and analytical
research support for antiterrorism efforts. The Bio-Terrorism Act Prior Notice Center, at NTC, will

Photo: Officers in primary inspection booth in El Paso, TX

target shipments that pose the highest risk for bio-terrorism. The NTC will integrate intelligence shared from vulnerability assessments conducted by USDA to implement agroterrorism rules in ATS to identify agricultural products with a high risk of intentional contamination. To broaden the scope of CBP targeting, NTC will work with other DHS components, law enforcement agencies and governments, expand its staff to better accommodate the ever-increasing demands for tactical information and continue to develop and refine more sophisticated targeting tools. CBP will implement Air AMS in phases, and in concert with this phased approach, the Automated Targeting System-Air (ATS-Air) will be fully deployed. The ability of the Automated Targeting System (ATS) to perform effective risk analysis will be strengthened through the deployment of four Screening and Targeting releases of the Automated Commercial Environment (ACE). The pilot for the Port Radiation Inspection, Detection and Evaluation (PRIDE), which serves as a conduit for all technical data collected at the ports, will be expanded to all detection devices at all ports of entry.

Objective 1.3

Strengthen the CBP defense-in-depth approach through the use of state-of-the-art detection and sensor technology, resources and training.

The goal of CBP is to screen 100 percent of all people, cargo and conveyances entering the United States based on national security threshold targeting and to examine all identified people, cargo and conveyances scoring above a mandatory threshold both abroad and at U.S. borders. Frontline officers and agents will use an array of radiation detection technology including personal radiation detectors (PRDs). CBP will build on existing non-intrusive inspection (NII) technology and expand the explosive and chemical detection canine program. To improve its ability to detect and deter

Photo: NII technology - truck passing through radiation portal at the port of Newark, NJ

illicit radiological materials and nuclear devices, CBP will develop and deploy highly integrated systems. CBP intends to identify emerging technologies, such as smart seals, using both passive detection and active inspection of cargo, to increase effectiveness for detecting illicit goods while speeding the flow of legitimate commerce.

Objective 1.4

Push the nation's zone of security outward beyond its physical borders through partnerships and extended border initiatives to deter and combat the threat of terrorism.

Working with foreign Attaché officers, foreign governments and the trade community, CBP will pre-screen and target shipments and containers that pose a potential risk for terrorism, before they arrive at United States ports of entry, using advance manifest information. The CBP Container Security Initiative (CSI) will establish a physical presence at foreign ports, share intelligence and leverage technology to enhance screening and examining containers. The Immigration Advisory Program (IAP) will deploy CBP inspectors to foreign airports to screen and interdict potential terrorists and inadmissible aliens. Through the Customs-Trade Partnership Against Terrorism (C-TPAT) voluntary program, CBP will partner with the trade community to secure global supply chains; develop secure, smart cargo containers; and establish minimum standards for cargo security. CBP will work with international organizations, such as the World Customs Organization (WCO) and the G8, and will continue to lead the international customs community in developing and ensuring the quick implementation of global standards governing supply chain security. In addition, CBP will promote cooperation through the Export Control and related Border Security (EXBS) assistance programs,

Photo: Hong Kong Seaport - In 2002, Hong Kong signed a CSI agreement with CBP

as well as other international training initiatives that focus on security and border enforcement. CBP will create smart borders through border accords with Canada and Mexico. The Free and Secure Trade (FAST) program will be extended to additional sites, while adding dedicated lanes at current FAST locations and expanding the program to air, rail and marine environments. In Canada, NEXUS-Highway, which allows expedited clearance to low-risk travelers, will be expanded to NEXUS-Air and NEXUS-Marine. Through coordinated operations (Air Bridge Denial/Joint Inter-Agency Task Force and Integrated Border Enforcement Teams (IBETs)), CBP will continue to work with its foreign government counterparts to increase detection and interdiction capabilities of people, goods and materials from the points of origin through their transit areas and eventually to their final destinations. Using cooperative agreements with countries in Central America, South America and the Caribbean, CBP will interdict air and marine smuggling conveyances before they reach United States borders.

Preventing Terrorism Between Ports of Entry

Strategic Goal Number 2

Strengthen control of the borders between the ports of entry to prevent the illegal entry of terrorists, terrorist weapons, contraband and illegal aliens into the United States.

To achieve this strategic goal, CBP will implement the National Border Patrol Strategy, which consists of five main objectives with the goal of establishing and maintaining operational control of the borders. The five objectives include: 1. Establish substantial probability of apprehending terrorists and their weapons as they attempt to illegally enter the United States; 2. Deter illegal entries through improved enforcement; 3. Apprehend and deter smugglers; 4. Leverage smart border technology to multiply the effect of enforcement personnel; and 5. Reduce crime in border communities and improve the quality of life and economic vitality of regions. To achieve these objectives, the CBP Border Patrol will employ a highly centralized and strengthened organizational model. The agency will maximize border security with an appropriate balance of personnel, equipment, technology, communications capabilities and tactical infrastructure. Further, CBP plans to expand the antiterrorism mission of the Border Patrol through a national command structure, partnerships, intelligence sharing, training, technology, infrastructure support and the use of specialized rapid-response teams.

Objective 2.1

Enhance the intelligence program, and improve intelligence-driven operations.

Photo by James Tourtellotte

Photo: Border Patrol agents patrol the waters of the Rio Grande River

To enable CBP to deploy its resources effectively targeting areas of greatest risk, the Border Patrol will expand the use of national security and terrorist-related intelligence and targeting information to improve intelligence-driven operations. These operations will be coordinated with the Office of Field Operations to ensure maximum effectiveness at and between the ports of entry. In order to support tactical and strategic operations, the Border Patrol will enhance its intelligence program by coordinating with the CBP Office of Intelligence. In addition, the CBP Border Patrol will leverage the intelligence capabilities of the Offices of Intelligence, Field Operations and Anti-Terrorism to increase threat assessment, targeting efforts, operational planning and communication to support its antiterrorism and traditional missions. The CBP Border Patrol will support the agricultural mission through cooperative, tactical assistance to prevent introduction of agricultural contraband between the ports.

Objective 2.2

Maximize border security, along the northern, southern and coastal borders, through an appropriate balance of personnel, equipment, technology, communications capabilities and tactical infrastructure.

Differing threats result from the diversity of the borders and require the CBP Border Patrol to maintain flexibility in its border security approach. To support border control efforts between the ports of entry, CBP will leverage technology, tactical infrastructure and facilities to maximize the effectiveness of Border Patrol agents. CBP intends to add remote monitoring technology along the borders, including deploying the America's Shield Initiative (ASI), which will improve the Border Patrol's ability to assess threats and determine likely illegal border entry scenarios and locations.

Southern Border:

CBP will employ rapid response capabilities; state-of-the-art technologies; intelligence, skills and training; and national deployment of personnel and materials. Through checkpoints, intelligence-driven special operations and targeted patrols, CBP will deter or deny access to urban areas, infrastructure, transportation and routes of egress to smuggling organizations. CBP aims to increase the use of mobile personnel, improve air and ground support, increase rapid response capabilities and expand inter-agency cooperation. Through the Arizona Border Control Initiative (ABCI), CBP aims to obtain greater operational control of the Arizona border.

Photo: Border Patrol agent monitoring cameras in El Centro, CA

Northern Border:

Ensuring sufficient mobile workforce levels, as well as testing, acquisition and deployment of sensing and monitoring platforms, will be crucial to operational control on the Northern Border. CBP also plans to acquire additional air assets and use checkpoints and other deterrents. Partnerships with Canadian law enforcement and intelligence officials, and officials from federal, state, local and tribal organizations, will be strengthened. CBP aims to expand existing Integrated Border Enforcement, Maritime and Intelligence Teams (IBET/IMET/IBIT) and improve intelligence sharing.

Coastal Border:

Using customs and immigration authorities and trusted marine programs, investing in air and maritime assets, enhancing cooperation with other law enforcement agencies, including the U.S. Coast Guard, and leveraging available assets will ensure CBP has flexible coastal response capabilities. CBP will establish a common operational picture, right-size the marine assets, prepare for mass migration incidents and analyze future vulnerabilities.

Objective 2.3

Expand specialized teams and rapid-response capabilities to enhance control of the borders with expansion to problematic areas as identified through continuing threat assessments.

CBP will expand the training and response capabilities of the Border Patrol's specialized BORTAC—

Photo: Border Patrol agents conducting BORTAC exercise in southwest Texas 25

Border Patrol National Tactical Unit; BORSTAR—Border Patrol Search, Trauma and Rescue Team; and Special Response Teams to support domestic and international intelligence-driven and antiterrorism efforts, as well as other special operations. These teams will assist in terrorism prevention through planning, training and tactical deployment. As a highly mobile, rapid-response tool, they will significantly increase the ability of CBP to respond operationally to specific terrorist threats and incidents, while supporting the traditional Border Patrol missions.

Objective 2.4

Develop a more flexible, well-trained, nationally directed program and address critical infrastructure, facility and technology needs.

CBP will use a national command structure to facilitate determinations on threat and resource priorities and allow the rapid deployment of assets. To meet the antiterrorism mission, CBP intends to assess and provide the necessary multi-disciplinary training, which will ensure that agents can effectively use the state-of-the-art technology and resources. CBP will also train agents to properly refer and seize agricultural contraband between the ports of entry. To ensure infrastructure needed to support the mission is available, CBP will evaluate and address infrastructure and facility needs. They include new construction; the preservation of buildings, vehicles and fences; and the deployment and maintenance of new technologies including remote cameras, computers and intelligence, as well as those included in the America's Shield Initiative.

Photo: BORSTAR team removes an injured person from the southwest Texas desert

Unifying As One Border Agency

Strategic Goal Number 3

Increase the security of the homeland by completing the merger and unification of all United States border agencies.

Photo by Gerald Nino

Photo: Commissioner Bonner pins the new CBP badge on Border Patrol agent Araceli Ortega

Objective 3.1

Create a shared law enforcement culture throughout the agency to secure the homeland.

CBP intends to build on the proud histories and traditions to move forward in its new shared mission and values. The agency aims to create a uniformed law enforcement workforce, that works together in a professional manner and with courtesy and respect towards the public, and that is recognized worldwide. Strong and dynamic training and hiring programs will assure that a proactive integrity program permeates throughout the agency. CBP intends to improve its processing capabilities and work as an integrated team. New uniform, badge (the first DHS law enforcement badges) and credential conversion initiatives will visibly demonstrate a unified face to the traveling public and trade.

Objective 3.2

Develop and implement policy, management, operations, infrastructure and training initiatives to integrate frontline border enforcement personnel.

CBP officers will be equipped with firearms, radiation detection pagers and other technologies necessary to carry out the mission. To ensure that appropriate coordination and required backup takes place, the agency will establish and maintain communication between CBP agents and officers. CBP will implement a standardized approach to pay administration and personnel policies. Labor and employee relations issues will be assessed, along with the need to acquire additional mission support staff and resources. The CBP officer of the future will be trained in agriculture, customs and immigration matters and capable of performing primary and secondary inspections, as well as specialized duties. New CBP agriculture specialists will be trained to fill vacancies nationwide. All personnel will have training in targeting and analysis, and skill set imbalances will be reconciled. Antiterrorism training will be critical to ensuring that Border Patrol agents are fully prepared to address the terrorism threat. CBP intends to upgrade to one compatible, integrated, automated information system and provide officers with needed access. Sharing among functional areas will maximize use of equipment and technology. All CBP canine programs and tactical radio communications capabilities will be integrated, and national interoperable capabilities will be provided to meet cross-operational needs between geographic areas. A new design of facilities will be implemented starting in airports around the country, to contain CBP primary and secondary inspection areas, and to combine functions previously performed by each legacy agency. Providing quick response capabilities in border enforcement areas will assure safety and enhance homeland security. The Border Patrol will continue to deploy assets to interior locations in the United States where

there is a direct nexus to border control operations such as transportation hubs, airports and bus stations to confront routes of egress for terrorists, smugglers and illegal aliens.

Objective 3.3

Establish a unified primary inspection process for passenger processing at all ports of entry into the United States and fully integrate analysis and targeting units.

The need for travelers to undergo three separate inspections for immigration, customs and agriculture has been eliminated. In all air and sea environments, CBP aims to increase the number of roving teams prior to primary inspection, and in baggage claim areas, and to establish Passenger Analysis Unit targets. CBP will cross-train officers so they can perform the majority of primary inspection work in one encounter with the traveler, reducing the average processing time for legitimate travelers and making better use of CBP resources. At airports, to streamline the passenger process within the CBP inspection area, the agency intends to modernize its facilities addressing the volume of passengers and cargo moving through the ports of entry, as well as accommodating significant staffing enhancements. To expedite the movement of international low-risk, frequent air travelers, an accelerated passenger system is under development to replace the Immigration and Naturalization Service Passenger Accelerated Service System (INSPASS). The new system will provide a single, integrated passenger processing system as an alternative primary inspection process for pre-approved, pre-screened eligible travelers.

Photo by Gerald Nino

Objective 3.4

Leverage the expertise, capabilities and legal authorities of CBP officers to establish antiterrorism secondary inspections.

Counter-Terrorism Response (CTR) teams will be increased and mandated at all ports of entry. The teams will include supervisors, and members of the Passenger Analytical Unit, Rover Teams and Anti-Terrorism Contraband Enforcement Teams. CBP will train the CTR teams, at all airports, seaports and land border facilities, in new fraudulent document detection, analytical skills and behavioral analysis capabilities. New facilities will be re-designed to collocate and merge secondary examination areas and appropriately locate needed equipment and technology. In addition, design and research is underway to create a unified secondary processing area equipped with cutting edge technology that addresses security concerns. CBP intends to increase the use of technology within its facilities to ensure that those who need to be in the secondary environment are properly monitored and arrive in the correct location. Systems will be updated and modified, in collaboration with US-VISIT and the accelerated passenger system, to assure that the data used to develop performance measures is collected consistently. This technology will result in better decision-making regarding admissibility of people and goods and facilitate the process for the majority of the population who do not require a secondary examination.

Photo by James Tourtellotte

Objective 3.5

Realign the Air and Marine Operations (AMO) to improve the overall operational effectiveness and efficiencies of CBP air and marine assets.

To realize greater operational effectiveness, the agency will realign the air and marine law enforcement personnel, missions and assets into CBP so that all assets operate effectively to support the border security mission. AMO will serve the interdiction and homeland security missions of CBP, as well as support U.S. Immigration and Customs Enforcement (ICE) investigations and other DHS requirements.

Photo: AMO pilots flying a Black Hawk helicopter 31

Facilitating Legitimate Trade and Travel

Strategic Goal Number 4

Facilitate the more efficient movement of legitimate cargo and people.

Objective 4.1

Modernize automated import, export and passenger processing systems to improve risk assessment and enforcement decision-making.

To improve risk assessment, CBP will use state-of-the-art modeling technologies to aid in the identity of high risk for commercial enforcement. CBP will develop and improve systems that can provide advance manifest information for pre-screening cargo containers, agricultural products and passengers. Trade and passenger related intelligence will be analyzed and distributed in a fast, meaningful way. Systems capable of linking law enforcement and other agency databases into one integrated database will be developed. To reduce redundancy and minimize impact on customer operations, CBP aims to develop automated systems to assist in inspection and examination. CBP plans to secure adequate resources to assure the continued development of the Automated Commercial Environment (ACE) and the International Trade Data System (ITDS). To improve enforcement decision-making, the Penalty Priority Trade Issue will be used to improve the effectiveness of the trade fraud process by emphasizing national direction, uniformity and swift action.

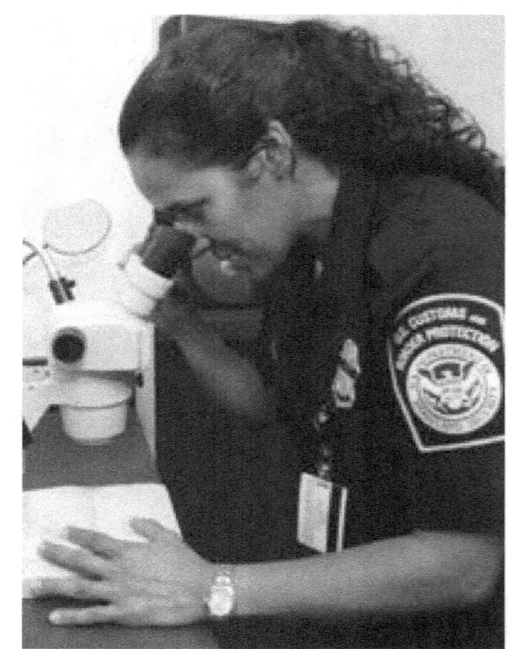

Photo by James Tourtellotte

Photo: CBP officers are expert in detecting fraudulent travel documents

Objective 4.2

Utilize state-of-the-art technologies and processes to leverage resources and to conduct examinations of all potential high-risk cargo, conveyances and passengers.

CBP will continue deploying non-intrusive inspection (NII) technology including radiation detection equipment, such as personal radiation detectors, radiation isotope identification devices and radiation portal monitors, as well as other screening technologies which support a layered inspection process. Facilitating low-risk travel, the agency will continue implementing more efficient inspection methods and technologies, such as NEXUS and SENTRI. In order to implement and enforce the 24-hour advance manifest rule, and expand the concept to additional industries and modes of transportation, CBP will persist in working with its trade partners. The provisions of the Immigration Reform Act will be enforced. CBP will leverage post-entry resources to effectively pursue trade enforcement risks. This expands enforcement efforts by CBP, beyond stopping trade at the border and conducting a physical cargo examination, to focus on entities involved in illicit business practices, trade fraud and non-compliance.

Photo: CBP officer using scanner to screen baggage   33

Objective 4.3

Promote industry and foreign government partnerships, by engaging foreign governments, the trade community and others in the supply chain in cooperative relationships, by ensuring that CBP matters are satisfactorily addressed in trade agreements and by guaranteeing that trading partners adhere to internationally accepted Customs standards.

To secure the vast international supply chain, CBP will enlarge the Container Security Initiative (CSI) to cover more cargo and locations. To increase maritime port security, the agency will work to internationalize C-TPAT through coordination with the international community. Supply chain security specialists will be hired and trained to visit participant facilities to review security practices. CBP intends to build on cooperative smart border agreements and pursue criminal enterprises involved in internal conspiracies at the ports of entry. CBP will implement critical action items of the Smart Border Accords with Canada and Mexico and expand FAST, NEXUS and SENTRI to expedite processing and secure the supply chain. The agency plans to continue improving trade compliance and enhancing partnership with the trade through the CBP Importer Self-Assessment Program. The Focused Assessment Program will help identify weaknesses indicating a potential risk of non-compliance. Through work with the World Customs Organization (WCO) and the G8, CBP will continue to lead the international customs community in developing and ensuring rapid implementation of global supply chain security standards. CBP will provide expert technical, legal and operational advice to agencies such as the Departments of Commerce and Agriculture, and the U.S. Trade Representative, on matters arising in trade agreements in support of the legal obligations of CBP to enforce, monitor and administer such agreements.

Photo: Commissioner Bonner and Sultan bin Sulayem sign a CSI agreement in Dubai

Objective 4.4

Enforce all U.S. trade, immigration, drug, consumer protection, intellectual property and agricultural laws and regulations at the borders.

The CBP National Trade Strategy will be implemented to provide a strategic approach to address trade risks with the appropriate level of resources while facilitating legitimate trade. The key principles guiding the actions and resources of the trade strategy include: focus on risk, leverage facilitation, enhance national oversight and multi-office cooperation and ensure revenue collection. CBP will integrate and balance its goals of trade facilitation and compliance using a consistent risk-based analytical approach organized around priority issues. Statistical data will be used to determine trade compliance. The validity of compliance measurement data will be strengthened to ensure that CBP border security targeting is based on accurate information. The agency will strengthen immigration and agricultural enforcement through cooperation with the U.S. Immigration and Customs Enforcement (ICE), U.S. Department of Agriculture (USDA) and other government agencies that have a stake in the traditional CBP mission areas. The overarching goal of working with other U.S. government agencies is to strongly encourage them to partner with CBP to adopt a broader, more comprehensive view of ways to leverage the risk management approach and to focus on high-risk and vulnerable areas. CBP will detect, interdict and refuse entry to prohibited plants, plant products, meat, meat by-products, live animals and endangered plant species. CBP intends to develop policies and procedures designed to enforce priority trade issues, improve enforcement of international trade agreements and respond to predatory trade practices that pose a risk to the public, the nation's economic stability and the ability of CBP to enforce trade laws and regulations.

Photo: Import specialist in Memphis, TN reviewing items imported into the United States   35

Objective 4.5

Facilitate international trade and travel.

To ensure that low-risk trade and travel receives expedited processing, CBP will improve and further develop the smart border concept. Trade partnership programs will be expanded to facilitate legitimate international trade while securing the supply chain. In order to gain support and input for key initiatives, CBP plans to continue reaching out to the international trade and transportation communities. Pre-enrollment programs will allow CBP to expedite processing of pre-screened and low-risk cargo and passengers, while high-risk cargo containers will be pre-screened prior to entering the country. The continued deployment of ACE/ITDS will ensure that legitimate trade will be expedited while the ability to effectively screen incoming cargo information is further strengthened. CBP will receive, track and issue timely, written and electronic rulings, enhance voluntary compliance through the issuance of Informed Compliance Publications and public outreach, as well as support and implement the Trade Adjustment Assistance Reform Act of 2002. ACE/ITDS expansion will allow more efficient tracking of financial transactions and bonding requirements, while ensuring that the collection of statistical information is significantly improved through direct collaboration with participating agencies such as the Census Bureau.

Photo: Commissioner Bonner and General Guzman-Montalvo of Mexico open a FAST lane in Laredo, TX

Photo by James Tourtellotte

Objective 4.6

Ensure revenue protection.

CBP will work to protect the revenue and use statistical data to measure its effectiveness in collecting revenue. The agency will develop strategies that maximize collection efforts for revenue owed the United States government under existing laws and regulations by ensuring that the CBP controls over the revenue process are keeping pace with changes in the trade environment. To protect the revenue, the agency will ensure that its policies are commensurate with the risk of financial exposure. CBP will perform periodic risk assessments to provide a reasonable assurance that material risks in the revenue process are being addressed. To ensure adequate protection for high-risk financial exposure, CBP will expand the use of bonding authority. The agency will also target areas of material revenue loss and use penalties to deter future non-compliance.

Photo: A lab technician tests the integrity of steel pipe as it enters the country   37

Protecting America and Its Citizens

Strategic Goal Number 5

Contribute to a safer America by prohibiting the introduction of illicit contraband, such as illegal drugs, counterfeit goods and other harmful materials and organisms, into the United States.

Objective 5.1

Capitalize on the use of information and intelligence to identify and target the CBP enforcement response to drug trafficking, illegal immigration and other illegal activities.

CBP will support the development and implementation of the US-VISIT system (U.S. Visitor and Immigrant Status Indication Technology system). To distribute intelligence and law enforcement information, formal liaison with key agencies will be maintained. The agency plans to conduct timely post-seizure analyses in order to develop new intelligence leads, which will be shared with the appropriate offices within CBP and DHS. Intelligence on drug trafficking organizations, and money laundering activities used to support their operations, will be analyzed and distributed within CBP and DHS. CBP will analyze aviation and maritime intelligence data for its border, airspace and law enforcement support operations. The agency will collect, analyze and share information and intelligence internally and externally in a timely, integrated, coordinated

Photo by Gerald Nino

Photo: Border Patrol agent processing alien in southern California

and operationally focused manner. CBP plans to continue using the Automated Targeting System (ATS) to review advance information, identify targets for inspection as part of the agency's layered inspection process and expand the use of ATS to all modes. The deployment of multi-modal manifest, and new screening and targeting tools within ACE, will ensure that all forms of transportation information are collected in advance and appropriately screened for enforcement concerns. CBP is intent on enhancing the capability of NTC to conduct trend and field analysis and on assuring that the NTC is staffed with a cross section of employees representing multiple functions and agencies. CBP will continue the Agriculture Quarantine Inspection results monitoring program and apply existing statistical methodologies such as COMPEX to develop a CBP agriculture commodity-monitoring program. Through risk assessment and analysis, and improved inter-agency cooperation, CBP will continue to develop strategies designed to detect and prevent both the intentional and unintentional contamination of imported agricultural products that would cause harm to the American public, American agriculture or the nation's economy.

Objective 5.2

Deploy automation, systems, tools and other technologies that can be used to pre-screen and identify smugglers and smuggled merchandise to increase interdiction and apprehension effectiveness.

Proven technologies, such as license plate readers (LPRs) and NII technology, will be used to interdict illegal goods and commodities. To increase the detection of illegal commodities concealed in various modes of transportation, such as vehicles, trucks or trains, additional NII technologies will be deployed. Using technology, the agency aims to enhance agriculture and quarantine exclu-

Photo: Secretary Chertoff looking through a fiber-optic scope at the Douglas port of entry   39

sion activities, as it reduces the threat of agricultural pests and diseases approaching the United States. Improving training and maintenance will enable CBP to maximize the use of operational high-tech equipment. CBP aims to expand the availability of applied technology and the capability of its research and development function to identify, develop and deploy systems to interdict illegal commodities.

Objective 5.3

Cooperate with other agencies, foreign governments and industry partners to administer and enforce the laws of the United States.

To exchange information, facilitate international interdiction efforts and support foreign assistance programs, CBP will expand international cooperation with foreign governments and enhance its partnerships within DHS and with other federal agencies. Foreign customs and law enforcement agencies will receive technical assistance and training from CBP enforcement and trade experts. Sanctions and embargoes against restricted foreign countries, imposed by the United States government, will be enforced. CBP intends to ensure that its trading partners comply with current United States export reporting requirements and that export transactions are properly authorized. Interagency task forces will target organizations and networks involved in the trafficking of stolen property. Working with foreign governments and the travel industry, CBP will implement the Immigration Advisory Program, stationing inspectors overseas to screen and interdict potential terrorists and inadmissible aliens to prevent them from boarding aircraft destined for the United States. CBP plans to continue expanding and using the Automated Export System (AES) to assist in tracking illegal exports with the agency's government partners. In conjunction with various foreign gov-

Photo: Canine inspecting boxes in a warehouse facility in Warrenton, VA

Photo by James Tourtellotte

ernments, CBP will continue to enhance international cooperation in identifying and enforcing trade issues related to Intellectual Property Rights (IPR), antidumping and textile and wearing apparel. The agency will also continue to conduct industry outreach to familiarize IPR holders on how to work with CBP to protect intellectual property at the border.

Objective 5.4

Reduce the importation of all prohibited or illegal drugs and other materials that are harmful to the public or may damage the American economy.

Functions or traditional missions transferred to DHS and CBP will not be diminished or neglected, except by Act of Congress. CBP will monitor connections between illegal drug trafficking and terrorism and coordinate efforts to sever such connections, while interdicting illegal narcotics. To reduce the risk of narcotics entering the United States, the agency plans to enhance industry partnerships. As part of Air Bridge Denial, Operation Halcon and other counter-narcotic operations, CBP will provide drug interdiction support to other governments. Canine resources will be used to detect illegal aliens, explosives and chemicals and to interdict drugs and agricultural commodities. Through an aggressive IPR strategy, CBP aims to reduce the importation of merchandise that could be harmful to the public or may damage the economy. The Strategy Targeting Organized Piracy (STOP) initiative will move CBP beyond the traditional transaction oriented physical exam approach to using new approaches geared to entities involved in business practices linked to counterfeiting and piracy. CBP intends to continue developing an IPR Risk Model to identify or predict imports and entities that have a potential to be at high risk for IPR violations. CBP will prevent prohibited items from entering U.S. borders and improve information exchange with private industry on exports of

Photo: CBP patrol officer with hundreds of pounds of marijuana from an undercover operation in Arizona 41

sensitive or controlled commodities. CBP intends to work closely with other government agencies, industry and stakeholders to measure agricultural risk and develop mitigation strategies to prevent harmful organisms, both intentional and unintentional, from entering the United States. CBP aims to continue its partnership with the Food and Drug Administration to enforce the Bio-terrorism Act and will use technological innovations to bolster its pest exclusion mission.

Objective 5.5

Provide support to protect events and key assets of national interest, and mitigate the risks of terrorism and other threats to critical Government operations.

CBP will continue to coordinate with the Department of Defense and other law enforcement partners to protect the National Capital Region from airborne threats. The agency will also support efforts to provide air and marine security for national events.

Photo: A Black Hawk helicopter on patrol to protect the Nation's capital

Modernizing and Managing

Strategic Goal Number 6

Build a strong, modern management infrastructure that assures the achievement of business results.

Photo: The CBP annual report of accomplishments and financial health

Financial, Acquisition and Asset Management

Objective 6.1

Improve budgeting and financial processes, policies and systems, ensuring accurate, reliable allocation of, and accounting for, expenditure of funds, collection of revenues and maintenance of reliable, timely and accurate financial data for decision-making and reporting.

Objective 6.2

Improve asset acquisition and management methods and procedures, ensuring the effective procurement of supplies, services and equipment in alignment with the CBP mission, goals

and priorities. Implement systems and processes to efficiently construct, maintain, distribute and dispose of assets needed to carry out the CBP operational missions.

CBP will assist its customers and stakeholders in obtaining and managing the financial resources and assets needed to accomplish the mission. To provide customers and stakeholders with accurate, timely and integrated data, CBP intends to maintain and improve financial and administrative systems, along with increasing the use of e-commerce. To aid understanding and use of financial management systems and procedures, CBP plans to provide improved training and assistance. To accommodate operational, staffing and security needs for CBP, the agency will continue to develop and implement a master plan for facility infrastructure improvements. CBP will also continue to refine and improve its acquisition methods in order to provide personnel with the personal property, fleet and services needed to do their job, while improving record-keeping, accountability, as well as control and maintenance of all property and assets.

Photo: CBP manages 165 land ports of entry in the United States, such as this one in Mariposa, AZ

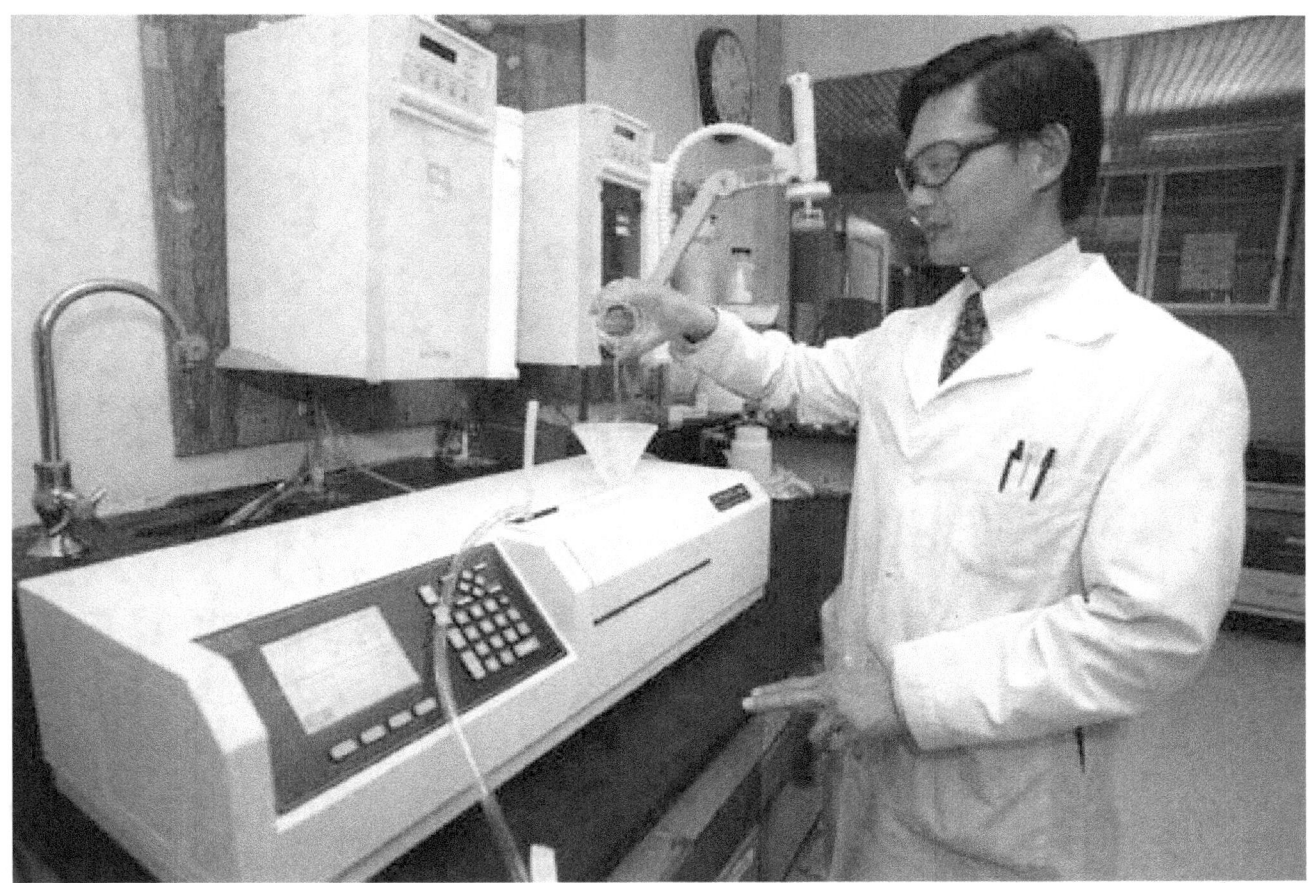

Information, Science and Technology

Objective 6.3

Develop and deploy innovative and secure systems and advanced technologies including ACE, APIS, US-VISIT, ATS, radiation portal monitors, NII systems and America's Shield Initiative to improve targeting and screening of goods, people and conveyances entering the United States.

Objective 6.4

Maintain a reliable, stable and secure IT infrastructure and an array of technical support services including laboratory and scientific services, tactical radio communication, field equipment maintenance/support and 24/7 customer assistance.

CBP will continue to support its antiterrorism mission and its widely dispersed field workforce by deploying a modern, robust, secure technology infrastructure providing global systems integration and information warehousing for a completely automated trade, border security and mission support environment. CBP intends to build and maintain a unified tactical communications capability that supports the needs of the agency and is coordinated within DHS. Also, in accordance with the Federal Information Security Management Act (FISMA) of 2002, CBP will ensure security of infor-

Photo: Lab technician conducting research   45

mation assets and maintain a CBP enterprise architecture consistent with the federal enterprise architecture (FEA) reference model structure and develop products and services using standard processes and innovative management tools.

Photo: Border Patrol agent checking fingerprints, San Diego Sector

Human Capital

Objective 6.5

Align human resources systems with the mission to ensure that recruitment, compensation, performance management, succession management and leadership of employees support professional, timely and effective service delivery to carry out the CBP mission.

Objective 6.6

Promote continued compliance with the nation's civil rights laws and federal regulations.

CBP will recruit, hire and retain a highly skilled and qualified workforce through national strategies that are targeted, tactical and consistent with operational needs. The Human Capital strategy will align with all aspects of mission, planning and budgeting, while human resources policies and programs will align with CBP goals and will be flexible. CBP management will benefit from improved methods for selecting and managing a high quality workforce, as well as a roster of cleared applicants to ensure timely staffing of positions. Workforce characteristics and future needs will support CBP achieving its goal of unifying as one border agency and take advantage of technological advances to address changes in core occupations. Through recruitment, development and suc-

Photo: Graduates of the first CBP officer training class at FLETC, Glynco, GA 47

cession management plans, CBP aims to ensure continuity of effective leadership. Customer hiring plans will identify the size, deployment and necessary competencies of future recruits. Performance measurement methods will support modern compensation and rewards systems. To attract and retain employees, the agency intends to obtain and use flexible recruitment authorities. Technology helps analyze workforce trends and automates human resource processes to conduct workforce analyses and develop succession management plans. The enhanced use of alternative dispute resolution will focus on education, prevention and resolution.

Photo: CBP officer and CBP Border Patrol agent saluting

Training and Development

Objective 6.7

Develop and implement training initiatives that support the agency mission and priority goals, objectives and strategies in the CBP Strategic Plan.

A National Training Plan will be implemented that links and prioritizes agency-wide training initiatives with CBP goals and prepares a multi-disciplinary workforce to unifying as one border agency. Reaching a widely dispersed and diverse workforce involves integrating technology-enabled systems for distance learning. A field-based training infrastructure will support the consistent, nationwide delivery of training at ports of entry and field offices. Joint training exercises will rehearse coordinated efforts of state, local and federal law enforcement officials to combat terrorists and terrorist weapons. To support enhanced border and homeland security responsibilities, CBP plans to administer to the tactical competency of armed officers. Career development programs for CBP mission-critical occupations, and essential leadership and supervisory training, will be offered. Training programs will be assessed based on priority needs, perceived value, return on investment and contribution to overall performance. A business case analysis process guides training investments. To create an air and marine workforce that is universally assignable to meet the mission, CBP will standardize air and marine training and develop a plan.

Photo: Firearms instructors oversee the firing line   49

Management Effectiveness

Objective 6.8

Conduct ongoing assessments of CBP operations to assure effective and efficient utilization of resources.

Through the President's Management Agenda (PMA), CBP will demonstrate its commitment to achieving results and outcomes and fostering a results-oriented organizational culture. The Performance Assessment Rating Tool (PART) will be utilized to determine the best use of resources. The budget decision process will be integrated with the CBP formal program review and performance measurement process, and the Future Year Homeland Security Program (FYHSP) system will be used to track and report on accomplishments. Performance measures will continuously be reviewed and revised to ensure that CBP measures are effective at demonstrating results.

Photo: An unmanned aerial vehicle (UAV) used by CBP along rugged areas of the U.S. border

Coordination with Other Agencies, Governments and the Private Sector

A basic foundation of the CBP Strategic Plan involves coordination, integration and cooperation to enforce hundreds of laws and regulations in partnership with numerous federal, state, local and tribal law enforcement agencies. The following are a few of the many efforts, which represent the commitment of CBP to fostering external cooperation and coordination with entities that can assist in protecting the homeland.

Other Agencies...

- CBP, in cooperation with the Departments of State, Defense and Energy, conducts hands-on training and provides other technical assistance to many high-risk countries on how to detect and interdict smuggling, particularly the smuggling of nuclear and radiological materials and sensitive technologies.

- CBP provides aviation support to FEMA and DHS officials in the aftermath of national emergencies, such as a terrorist attack, hurricane, tornado or other natural disaster, allowing immediate disaster assessments by FEMA personnel on board and providing digital videos for viewing by officials on the ground. CBP aircraft also transport the FEMA Rapid Needs Assessment Teams and perform a variety of humanitarian aid and relief flights.

- CBP works jointly with the Federal Aviation Administration, Department of Defense, the Secret Service and the Transportation Security Administration to provide airspace security over the Nation's Capital to protect America's leadership against a terrorist attack.

- CBP and the Food and Drug Administration have cooperated to establish operational procedures for implementation of the Public Health Security and Bioterrorism Preparedness and Response Act (BTA) of 2002. The BTA was enacted to protect the citizens and economy of the United States from the intentional contamination of imported food. The Prior Notice Center was created at the CBP National Targeting Center to enhance the targeting of imported food shipments for bioterrorism.

- CBP works closely with the U.S. Department of Agriculture (USDA) on vulnerability assessments designed to identify points in the production of imported agricultural products where biological, chemical and radiological contaminants could be intentionally added to foods. CBP and USDA are developing rule sets for implementation in ATS for the targeting of agricultural products with a risk of intentional contamination.

- CBP is an integral part of the International Trade Data System (ITDS) effort, which is working with 24 participating government agencies to consolidate the collection of security and trade information within the Automated Commercial Environment (ACE) platform.

- CBP is working with Immigration and Customs Enforcement to enhance the Student Exchange Visitor Information System processing at the ports of entry. In addition, CBP has established a Fraud Detection Unit to work closely with the Forensic Document Laboratory. CBP and U.S. Citizenship and Immigration Services have combined efforts to coordinate parole and immigrant visa procedures.

- CBP has established Memorandums of Understanding with the Department of Energy and the National Nuclear Security Administration to formalize the ongoing exchange of information and collaborative working relationships.

- CBP facilitates the exchange of information and intelligence and shares resources through the Integrated Border Enforcement Team, a partnership with federal, state and local United States agencies, as well as the Royal Canadian Mounted Police.

Foreign Governments...

- CBP launched the Container Security Initiative (CSI) in January 2002, which, through partnerships with its foreign counterparts, is designed to help protect global trade lanes by targeting and examining shipments that pose a threat, as early as possible in the global supply chain.

- SENTRI, or Secure Electronic Network for Traveler's Rapid Inspection, is an automated, dedicated

commuter lane, which provides a more efficient means of traffic management, thereby reducing congestion and accelerating the inspections of certain low-risk pre-enrollees at ports of entry.

- NEXUS, an alternative inspection program, allows pre-screened, low-risk travelers to be processed with little or no delay by United States and Canadian border officials.

- CBP provides aviation support for drug interdiction operations in source and transit zones in Central and South America through the Joint Interagency Task Force.

- CBP is actively engaged with numerous foreign nations in establishing modernization and capacity building programs to develop further customs operational and border security capabilities.

- CBP, through international forums such as the World Customs Organization, is actively promoting the internationalization of common data elements, supply chain security standards, industry partnership programs, as well as other customs issues to achieve a common platform across all customs administrations.

The Private Sector...

- CBP has developed partnerships with the trade community under the Customs-Trade Partnership against Terrorism (C-TPAT). This is the largest public/private sector partnership to arise out of 9/11, designed to enhance security and trade facilitation in the supply chain.

- In partnership with the private sector, and the governments of Canada and Mexico, CBP developed FAST, or the Free and Secure Trade program. FAST provides for expedited cargo processing between the United States, Canada and Mexico for carriers, importers and commercial drivers that are recognized as securing themselves against terrorist vulnerabilities.

- CBP maintains an outreach program, via the Office of Trade Relations, the Trade Symposium and the Commercial Operations Advisory Committee (COAC), to ensure that the international trade and

transportation community understands the agency's mission and goals and to obtain their input on legal, operational and policy concerns. This collaboration enables CBP to incorporate feedback from the private sector into key initiatives, lessens the impact of new programs on industry and ensures that CBP and the trade advance together toward a common goal.

- CBP works closely with commercial airlines to develop and further expand the Advanced Passenger Information System (APIS), which processes passenger manifests for inbound international air passengers and works with the Coast Guard and the Transportation Security Administration to examine crew lists.

These efforts represent the commitment by CBP to fostering external cooperation and coordination with stakeholders. As CBP implements its Strategic Plan, this commitment to cooperation will play a critical role in achieving its strategic goals.

In the future, CBP, as well as the other organizations within DHS, must answer the challenge placed before it to be a proactive leader in the fight against terrorism. New strategies, technologies, partnerships and resources are needed to deter, detect and interdict. As one of the key operative agencies of the Department of Homeland Security, new opportunities will arise for CBP to enhance its capability to carry out the mission and to work more closely with others involved in protecting the homeland.

Photo: Commissioner Bonner speaks at the opening of the 5th annual Trade Symposium   53

Linking the Strategic Plan to Business Results

Through the Strategic Plan, CBP strives to maintain the focus created by the Government Performance and Results Act (GPRA); improving program efficiency and effectiveness, maintaining a results-oriented focus, clearly describing the goals and objectives of programs and developing a means of measuring progress. Developing an integrated planning methodology that is supported by meaningful performance measures is a primary focus toward demonstrating business results.

CBP is continuously refining and improving its performance measures and the data integrity and confidence of these measures. CBP validates its performance data through the assignment of a data element owner or through an established data quality control group. Data element owners are responsible for ensuring the quality and validity of the data. The accountable data owner is responsible for defining the element, the source(s) of the data, the reporting cycles for each element and the specific verification and validation method(s) for each data element. Quality control is also achieved through data reviews to ensure accuracy by reviewing collection procedures, as well as reviewing data for any anomalies.

In general, CBP verifies and validates its data via an array of internally and externally assessed methods. These include management inspections, Headquarters and field reviews, automated edits, program reviews, other agency validation, private sector feedback, independent audits and reviews, and Inspector General and Government Accountability Office audits.

It is often difficult to measure quantitatively how well law enforcement is meeting its challenges. CBP is no exception. The direct impact being made on unlawful activity is often unknown. This is particularly true in the case of counter-terrorism and narcotics trafficking efforts. The totality of violations is difficult to estimate, and therefore the impact of the agency's efforts is often difficult to state in quantifiable terms. Because of these and other unknown variables, the traditional economics and methodologies of measuring performance for law enforcement can be particularly challenging. Where possible, measures that show the impact of CBP efforts have been developed. CBP, in cooperation with supporting agencies, continues to address and explore these issues in an effort to improve the scope and breadth of its measurement tools.

Baseline performance metrics are identified and addressed through periodic revisions to the CBP Annual Performance Plan and internal program planning and budget documents. The Strategic Plan and the Performance Plan both cross-reference to one another and also serve as the framework for other planning and organizational documents.

CBP is constantly improving its performance measure framework and has identified organizational measures, as well as measures used to manage programs internally. The Strategic Plan includes examples of a number of CBP performance measures. They are used by programs to measure incrementally the overall performance of the programs and how well they are achieving success. In addition, CBP regularly reviews, updates and reports on the measures contained in FYHSP to ensure that measures effectively demonstrate results.

Performance Measures

The following definitions are used for CBP performance measurement methodology:

Outcome measure:

An indicator that measures the agency-wide effect or results of the programs or services provided.

Output measure/workload indicator:

An indicator that measures the quantity of a service or good produced and/or pertains to external drivers that require a task or activity to be performed.

Efficiency measure:

An indicator that measures inputs used per unit of output (i.e. waiting times).

Input measure:

An indicator that measures units of resources expended to produce services (i.e. cost of operations).

The following chart provides a representative sample of CBP performance measures. CBP continues to evaluate and update the measures. A complete list of measures is contained in the DHS and CBP Annual Performance Plans.

Relationships Between FY 2006 Performance Measures & CBP Goals

CBP Goal #1: Preventing Terrorism at the Ports of Entry

Performance Measure	Type of Measure
Number of foreign mitigated examinations by category (CSI)*	Outcome Measure
Percent of worldwide U.S. destined containers processed through CSI ports*	Outcome Measure
Number of CSI operational ports*	Output Measure
Targeting efficiency ratio (TER) in the air passenger environment*	Efficiency Measure
Targeting efficiency ratio (TER) in the land passenger environment*	Efficiency Measure

CBP Goal #2: Preventing Terrorism Between the Ports of Entry

Performance Measure	Type of Measure
Border miles under operational control	Outcome Measure
Increase agent time on linewatch*	Efficiency Measure

CBP Goal #3: Unifying as One Border Agency

Performance Measure	Type of Measure
Total number of linked electronic sources from CBP and other government agencies for targeting information*	Outcome Measure

CBP Goal #4: Facilitating Legitimate Trade and Travel

Performance Measure	Type of Measure
Percent of travelers compliant (air passenger environment)*	Outcome Measure
Percent of travelers compliant (vehicle passenger environment)*	Outcome Measure
APIS data sufficiency rate*	Outcome Measure
Reduction in lost revenue: trade	Outcome Measure
Average cost per CSI port to achieve operational status*	Efficiency Measure
Compliance rate for C-TPAT members with established C-TPAT guidelines*	Outcome Measure
Average CBP exam reduction ratio for C-TPAT member importers*	Outcome Measure
C-TPAT validation labor efficiency rate*	Efficiency Measure
Time savings to process U.S./Mexico border FAST lane transactions*	Efficiency Measure
Percent of truck and rail containers examined using NII*	Outcome Measure
Percent of sea containers examined using NII*	Outcome Measure
Average wait time*	Efficiency Measure
Percent of internal population using ACE functionality to manage trade information*	Outcome Measure

CBP Goal #5: Protecting America and Its Citizens

Performance Measure	Type of Measure
International air passenger compliance with agricultural quarantine regulations*	Outcome Measure
Border vehicle passengers in compliance with agricultural quarantine regulations*	Outcome Measure
Number of pounds of cocaine seized (at the ports)*	Output Measure
Number of pounds of marijuana seized (at the ports)*	Output Measure
Number of pounds of heroine seized (at the ports)*	Output Measure
Percentage of no-launches to prevent acts of terrorism and other illegal activities (AMO)*	Outcome Measure
Number of launches not completed within the targeted time frame of request to launch for the alert aircraft	Outcome Measure

CBP Goal #6: Modernizing and Managing

Performance Measure	Type of Measure
Operational requirements-based budgeting program*	Outcome Measure
Percent of trade accounts with access to ACE functionality to manage trade information*	Efficiency Measure
Percentage of electronically processed duties, taxes and fees collected by ACE from trade accounts*	Efficiency Measure
Percent of time the TECS is available to end-users*	Outcome Measure
Cost-per-transaction to ensure TECS availability to end-users	Efficiency Measure

* This FYHSP measure corresponds to more than one CBP strategic goal. This goal was chosen as the primary goal because more objectives were aligned within this strategic goal than in any other goal.

Use of Program Evaluations within CBP

Program evaluations complement the use of performance measures in assessing program effectiveness. Using both objective measurement and systematic analysis, program evaluations assist in determining if programs achieve the intended objectives. Program evaluations also assess program implementation processes and operating policies and practices when implementation rather than program outcome is a concern.

CBP uses various approaches to conducting program evaluations. These approaches include:

- Internal reviews conducted by individual CBP program offices
- Internal reviews managed by CBP with the assistance of outside consultants
- Management inspections conducted by CBP Management Inspection Division
- Reviews and audits performed by the Office of the Inspector General
- Reviews and audits performed by the Government Accountability Office

The following table summarizes the program evaluations used to develop the Strategic Plan and the program evaluations proposed to implement the Plan.

Program Evaluations Used to Develop the Plan

Strategic Goal	Evaluation Area	Explanation/Focus
Preventing Terrorism At Ports of Entry	Homeland Security: Limited Progress in Deploying Radiation Detection Equipment At U.S. Ports Of Entry (GAO-03-963)	Radiation Detection Equipment
	Homeland Security: Challenges Remain in the Targeting of Oceangoing Cargo Containers for Inspection (GAO-04-352)	Cargo Container Processing - Domestic
	Protecting the Public: Security, Inspection and Targeting of Vessel Containers at U.S. Seaports Can Be Improved (OIG-03-074)	Customs Inspection of Vessel Containers at Major Seaports - National
	An Evaluation of the Security Implications of the Visa Waiver Program (OIG-04-26)	Visa Waiver Program
Preventing Terrorism Between Ports of Entry	Border Security: Agencies Need to Better Coordinate Their Strategies and Operations on Federal Lands (GAO-04-590)	Land Management Agencies Border Issues
	INS' Southwest Border Strategy: Resource and Impact Issues Remain After Seven Years (GAO-01-842)	Illegal Immigration Southwest Border Strategy
Unifying As One Border Agency	Land Border Ports of Entry: Vulnerabilities and Inefficiencies in the Inspections Process (GAO-03-782NI)	Illegal Alien Entry at Land Border Ports
	Comparison of INS and Customs Premium and Overtime Pay Systems (GAO-02-21)	INS and Customs Premium and Overtime Pay Systems
	Customs and INS: Random Inspection Programs Can Be Strengthened (GAO-02-215R)	Random Inspection Program

Program Evaluations Used to Develop the Plan

Strategic Goal	Evaluation Area	Explanation/Focus
Facilitating Legitimate Trade and Travel	International Trade: U.S. Customs and Border Protection Faces Challenges in Addressing Illegal Textile Transshipment (GAO-04-345)	Textile Transshipment Monitoring
	Intellectual Property: U.S. Efforts Have Contributed to Strengthened Laws Overseas. But Challenges Remain (GAO-04-912)	IPR Enforcement
	Trade and Passenger Processing: Customs IPR Enforcement Strategy and Management Controls Over the IPR Module Need to Be Strengthened (OIG-03-027)	Intellectual Property Rights Enforcement
	Revenue Collection: Enhanced Controls Could Prevent Improper Payment of Customs Drawback Claims (OIG-03-026)	Drawback Claims Processing
	Container Security: Expansion of Key Customs Programs Will Require Greater Attention to Critical Success Factors (GAO-03-770)	Cargo Container Processing - Foreign Point of Origin
Protecting America and Its Citizens	Passenger Processing: Changes to the Advance Passenger Information System Have Been Made but Its Value As An Enforcement Tool is Dependent on Factors Outside (OIG-03-059)	Advance Passenger Information System (APIS)
	Protecting the Public: Security, Inspection and Targeting of Vessel Containers at U.S. Seaports Can Be Improved (OIG-03-074)	Customs Inspection of Vessel Containers at Major Seaports
	Trade Processing: The National HAZMAT Program Needs to Be Strengthened (OIG-03-065)	Hazardous Material (HAZMAT) Program
	U.S. Customs Service Intelligence Program (OIG-01-065)	Customs Intelligence Program
Modernizing and Managing	Revenue Protection: Customs Is Not Collecting All Revenue Due From International Mail (OIG-02-020)	International Mail
	Interim Report on Customs ACE Program Management: Customs Needs to Adequately Staff the Modernization Office (OIG-02-058)	Automated Customs Enforcement (ACE)
	Financial Management: Review of the U.S. Customs Service's Fiscal Year 2001 Financial Statements (OIG-02-073)	Customs Financial Process FY '01 Financial Statements
	Protecting the Public: U.S. Customs' Control Over Sensitive Property Needs to Be Improved (OIG-02-109)	Customs Inventory Practices

Program Evaluation Proposed to Implement the Plan

Strategic Goal	Evaluation Area	Explanation/Focus
Preventing Terrorism At Ports of Entry	Level 1, Level 2 and Level 3 Antiterrorism and Comprehensive Port Inspections	Various Ports Based on Workload Volume and Previous Inspection Results
	Tier 1 and Tier 2 Antiterrorism Focused Program Reviews	Various Program Areas Based on Homeland Security Mission Criticality and Identified Vulnerabilities
	Tier 1 Self-inspection Cycle	All Offices, Ports and Sectors Assess Compliance with CBP National Programs and Policies
Preventing Terrorism Between Ports of Entry	Border Patrol Sector Inspections	Various Northern, Southern and Coastal Sectors Based on Threat, Vulnerability and Operating Environments
	Tier 1 Self-inspection Cycle	All Offices, Ports and Sectors Assess Compliance with CBP National Programs and Policies
Unifying As One Border Agency	Level 1 and Level 2 Antiterrorism Focused Program Reviews	Various Program Areas Based on Homeland Security Mission Criticality and Identified Vulnerabilities
	Tier 3 Mission Critical Focused Program Reviews	Various Program Areas Based on Critical and Traditional Mission Program and Identified Vulnerabilities
	Tier 4 Administrative or Financial Programs/ Functions Focused Program Reviews	Various Program Areas Based on Critical and Traditional Mission Program and Identified Vulnerabilities
Facilitating Legitimate Trade and Travel	Level 1, Level 2 and Level 3 Antiterrorism and Comprehensive Port Inspections	Various Ports Based on Workload Volume and Previous Inspection Results
	Tier 1 and Tier 2 Antiterrorism Focused Program Reviews	Various Program Areas Based on Homeland Security Mission Criticality
	Tier 3 Mission Critical Focused Program Reviews	Various Program Areas Based on Critical and Traditional Mission Program and Identified Vulnerabilities
	Tier 1 and Tier 2 Self-inspection Cycle	All Offices, Ports and Sectors Assess Compliance with CBP National Programs and Policies
Protecting America and Its Citizens	Tier 3 Mission Critical Focused Program Reviews	Various Program Areas Based on Critical and Traditional Mission Program and Identified Vulnerabilities
	Tier 1 and Tier 2 Self-inspection Cycles	All Offices, Ports and Sectors Assess Compliance with CBP National Programs and Policies
Modernizing and Managing	Tier 4: Administrative or Financial Programs/ Functions Focused Program Reviews	Various Program Areas Based on Critical and Traditional Mission Program and Identified Vulnerabilities
	Tier 2 and Tier 3 Self-inspection Cycles	All Offices, Ports and Sectors Assess Compliance with CBP National Programs and Policies

Customs and Border Protection: Looking to the Future

2005 ●————————————→ 2010

	Goals	Results
Preventing Terrorism At Ports of Entry	Expand use of intelligence	Timely interdiction and enforcement actions
	Improve information and targeting	Increased use of targeting
	Use state-of-the-art technology	Increased detection of illicit goods
	Extend zone of security through partnerships	Zone of security extended beyond physical U.S. borders
Preventing Terrorism Between Ports of Entry	Enhance intelligence program	Effective deployment of resources to high-risk areas
	Implement comprehensive border strategy	Achieve operational control between ports of entry
	Expand rapid-response capabilities	Increased capability to respond to threats and incidents
	Address training and infrastructure needs	Effective use of technology, resources and infrastructure
Unifying As One Border Agency	Create a shared culture	Professional, courteous law enforcement workforce
	Resolve administrative issues	Integrated, fully skilled, highly trained officers
	Establish unified primary inspections	Single, unified inspection process
	Establish antiterrorism secondary inspections	Increased and enhanced secondary inspection process
	Realign air and marine operations	Greater operational effectiveness
Facilitating Legitimate Trade and Travel	Modernize processing systems	Improved trade risk assessment and enforcement
	Utilize state-of-the-art technologies and processes	Trade enforcement risks pursued
	Promote industry and foreign partnerships	Secure international supply chain
	Enforce laws and regulations	Laws and regulations enforced
	Develop smart border concept	Expedited international trade/travel and secure supply chain
	Ensure revenue protection/collection	Revenue collection efforts maximized
Protecting America and Its Citizens	Utilize information and intelligence	Enhanced targeting of illegal immigration and contraband
	Deploy technologies as force multiplier	Increased interdictions and apprehensions
	Cooperate with other entities	Enhanced partnerships facilitating interdiction
	Reduce importation of prohibited/illegal items	Reduced threat to public and critical infrastructure
	Provide air and marine support	Key events and assets protected
Modernizing and Managing	Maintain financial integrity	Performance/evaluation based decisions
	Improve asset management	Well managed assets
	Deploy innovative and secure IT systems	Modern, secure IT infrastructure
	Recruit, hire and retain qualified workforce	Skilled, high-quality, diverse workforce
	Deliver high-quality, cost-effective, mission-driven training	Well-trained, multi-disciplined workforce

Looking to the Future

Since 9/11, CBP has protected the nation with its pioneering smart border and extended border strategies and has protected the economy as well. CBP has done this – and will continue to do this – by moving forward on the initiatives set in motion after 9/11 – obtaining advance information of cargo and people (the 24-Hour and Trade Act Rules and APIS); developing the Automated Targeting Systems located at the CBP National Targeting Center; through the Container Security Initiative (CSI) and the Immigration Advisory Program (IAP); the Customs-Trade Partnership Against Terrorism (C-TPAT); and through trusted traveler programs, such as NEXUS, SENTRI and NEXUS AIR. These initiatives have helped to secure the borders without unduly impeding legitimate trade and travel, so important to the economy.

Working with private-sector partners, CBP is taking these partnerships to the next level by better defining the security criteria expected and the CBP benefits that flow from meeting the C-TPAT supply chain security requirements. In addition, CSI now operates in 36 of the largest foreign ports of the world, and the agency will continue reaching out to other countries to secure trade headed for the United States.

As CBP moves ahead, it will pioneer a new trusted air passenger program to replace INS PASS. Only individuals who are vetted and determined to pose no security, smuggling or illegal migration threat will be admitted and they will be biometrically identified upon arrival. The benefit will be expedited processing through CBP for immigration and customs clearance.

Technology will play an even greater role in helping CBP carry out its missions. CBP is making progress in modernizing its IT systems, such as ACE, the Automated Commercial Environment, to provide one window in government for all trade data. The agency is employing IT system technology to better target high-risk cargo and travelers entering the United States, and CBP is deploying more technology at the ports of entry and between the ports of entry to help detect potential criminals, terrorists and terrorist weapons, including weapons of mass destruction, such as radiological and nuclear weapons materials. CBP is pioneering the use of unmanned aerial vehicles to establish an aerial patrol of significant segments of the United States border to better detect intrusions, and the agency will implement important initiatives, like America's Shield Initiative, that will provide intrusion detection at virtually the entire land border with Mexico and Canada. This will be coupled with rapid response capabilities by the CBP Border Patrol to apprehend those who attempt to illegally enter the United States. The Border Patrol will be more mobile and responsive than ever before. This will allow CBP to bring all segments of the border under control. It will also reduce the overall number of illegal aliens coming into the country, which, in turn, will increase national security by making apprehension highly probable at all corridors of the border.

The goal of CBP for now and the foreseeable future is nothing short of gaining operational control of the borders in order to protect the homeland from terrorists and terrorist weapons. At the same time, CBP must also prevent terrorist penetration through the ports of entry. That is the importance of one border agency for this nation. CBP must protect the nation both at and between the ports of entry.

The job of CBP is not easy, but it is surely one of the most important jobs of any agency of the federal government. Americans look to the frontline law enforcement officers – to CBP employees – to protect the homeland and their economic way of life. This 2005–2010 CBP Strategic Plan will ensure that CBP fulfills this critical role.